FURRY LOVE NURTURING YOUR PET WITH TENDER LOVING CARE

KHUSHDIL MIR

Made with ♥ on the Notion Press Platform
www.notionpress.com

This book is dedicated to all the loving pet owners who provide their furry friends with the care, love, and attention they deserve.

Contents

Foreword

As a long-time pet owner and advocate, I am honored to write the foreword for this comprehensive guide to pet care. The author has expertly covered all the essential topics related to pet ownership, from understanding your pet's behavior and providing essential care, to engaging in pet-friendly activities and coping with loss. I highly recommend this book to both experienced and new pet owners, as it is an invaluable resource for ensuring a happy, healthy, and fulfilling life for you and your pet.

Preface

As a pet owner, I understand the joy and love that pets bring into our lives. However, I also know that caring for a pet can be a complex and sometimes overwhelming task. That's why I wrote this book, to provide a comprehensive and easy-to-follow guide to pet care. Whether you are a seasoned pet owner or a newcomer to the world of pet care, this book is designed to give you the information and support you need to ensure that you and your pet have a happy and healthy life together.

Preface

Prologue

Pets have been a cherished part of human life for thousands of years. From the loyal dogs who guarded our homes and herded our livestock, to the gentle cats who kept us company and chased away the mice, pets have been a constant source of love, comfort, and joy in our lives. In this book, we will explore the world of pet care and provide practical advice and tips for ensuring a happy and healthy life for you and your pet.

Acknowledgements

I would like to extend my heartfelt thanks to all those who have supported me in the creation of this book. To my family and friends, who have always encouraged me to follow my passion for pets, and to the many pet owners who have shared their stories and experiences with me, thank you for your love and support.

CHAPTER ONE

Introduction to Pet Care

Pets are more than just animals, they are members of our family. As pet owners, we have a responsibility to provide them with love, attention, and proper care. Pet care is an important aspect of pet ownership, and it is essential to ensure the health, happiness, and well-being of our furry friends.

In this chapter, we will explore why pet care is so important, and what benefits pet ownership can bring to our lives. We will also examine the responsibilities of pet ownership, and what it means to provide a loving and nurturing home for our pets.

Pet care is essential for many reasons. Proper nutrition, exercise, and health care help ensure that our pets stay healthy and happy. This not only enhances the quality of their lives, but also prolongs their life expectancy. Additionally, a well-cared for pet is more likely to exhibit positive behaviors and a happy disposition, making them more enjoyable companions.

Pet ownership can also bring many benefits to our lives. Studies have shown that pet ownership can lower stress levels, improve our mood, and increase physical activity.

Pets can provide us with a sense of purpose and fulfillment, and they can be great sources of comfort during difficult times.

However, pet ownership also comes with responsibilities. As pet owners, we must be committed to providing our pets with proper care and attention, and to creating a safe and comfortable environment for them. This includes providing nutritious food, daily exercise, and regular visits to the vet.

Pet care is a crucial aspect of pet ownership. By providing our pets with proper care, we can enhance their quality of life, improve our own well-being, and build strong, loving bonds with our furry friends. In this book, we will explore pet care in depth, and provide you with the tools and information you need to raise a healthy and happy pet.

Pets have a special place in our hearts and homes, and for good reason. They bring joy, love, and companionship into our lives, and they can provide us with many benefits that we may not have even considered.

In this section, we will explore some of the many benefits of pet ownership, and why having a pet can be such a rewarding experience.

1. Improved Physical Health: Owning a pet can encourage physical activity and exercise, which can help improve our overall health and well-being. Whether it's going for a walk with your dog, or playing with your cat, pets can help us stay active and healthy.
2. Mental Health Benefits: Pets can have a positive impact on our mental health. Studies have shown that pets can reduce stress, anxiety, and depression, and they can provide us with a sense of comfort and security.

3. Social Interaction: Pets can also provide opportunities for social interaction and bonding. Whether you're at the dog park, or simply talking to other pet owners, having a pet can help you meet new people and form new relationships.
4. Sense of Purpose: Pets can also provide us with a sense of purpose and fulfillment. Caring for a pet can help us feel needed and valued, and can give us a sense of accomplishment.
5. Increased Happiness: Pets can bring joy and happiness into our lives. Whether it's the wag of a dog's tail, or the purr of a cat, pets can bring a smile to our faces and brighten our days.

Pet ownership can bring many benefits to our lives. By providing us with opportunities for exercise, social interaction, and emotional support, pets can enhance our overall health and well-being. Whether you're a first-time pet owner, or a seasoned pro, the benefits of pet ownership are undeniable.

Pets bring joy and love into our lives, but they also come with responsibilities. As pet owners, it is our duty to provide our furry friends with proper care and attention, and to create a safe and comfortable environment for them.

In this section, we will explore the various responsibilities that come with pet ownership, and what it means to be a responsible pet owner.

1. Proper Nutrition: Providing your pet with a balanced and nutritious diet is one of the most important responsibilities of pet ownership. This involves selecting the right type and amount of food, as well as ensuring that your pet has access to clean water at all

times.

2. Regular Exercise: Regular exercise is important for your pet's physical and mental health. This can include daily walks, playtime, and other physical activities that are appropriate for your pet's breed and size.
3. Regular Health Care: Regular visits to the vet, as well as vaccinations and parasite control, are essential for your pet's health and well-being. Keeping up with regular check-ups and preventative care can help keep your pet healthy and prevent potential health problems.
4. Training and Socialization: Providing your pet with training and socialization opportunities can help ensure that they behave well in different situations and are well-adjusted to the world around them.
5. Financial Commitment: Pet ownership can be expensive, and it's important to be prepared for the financial costs involved, such as food, veterinary care, and supplies.
6. Time and Attention: Lastly, pets require time and attention from their owners. This includes providing daily playtime and affection, as well as regular grooming and cleaning.

Pet ownership is a big responsibility, but it can also be incredibly rewarding. By being a responsible pet owner and providing your pet with proper care and attention, you can build a strong, loving bond with your furry friend and ensure their health and happiness.

CHAPTER TWO

Understanding Your Pet

When it comes to pet ownership, there are many different options to choose from. From dogs and cats, to birds and reptiles, the variety of pets available can be overwhelming. Understanding the different types of pets available can help you make an informed decision about which type of pet is right for you and your lifestyle.

Dogs are one of the most popular pets and for good reason. They are known for their loyalty, affection, and trainability, and they come in a wide range of breeds and sizes, each with its own unique personality and characteristics. From small lap dogs to large working breeds, dogs can make great companions for people of all ages and lifestyles. They thrive on interaction and attention, and they need plenty of exercise to keep them physically and mentally healthy.

Cats are another popular pet choice, and are known for their independence and playful personalities. They are low-maintenance pets that are well-suited for apartment living, and they come in a variety of breeds and coat types. Cats are natural hunters, and they enjoy playing with toys and exploring their environment. They are also great companions for those who prefer a more relaxed and independent pet.

Birds can make great pets, and they come in a variety of species, from parakeets and canaries, to larger species like parrots and cockatiels. Birds are social creatures that require daily interaction and attention, and they can provide their owners with a unique and beautiful musical experience. Birds also come in a variety of colors and personalities, and they can be trained to do simple tricks and respond to commands.

Fish are popular pets that are easy to care for and can add a touch of tranquility to any home. From small goldfish to large tropical fish, there are many different species of fish to choose from, each with its own unique characteristics and requirements. Fish are great for those who are looking for a low-maintenance pet, as they do not require much attention or interaction, and they are easy to care for with the right equipment and setup.

Reptiles, such as snakes, lizards, and turtles, are exotic pets that are becoming increasingly popular. They require specialized care, including specific temperature and lighting requirements, but they can be fascinating pets to observe and interact with. Reptiles are great for those who are interested in exotic creatures, and they can provide a unique and interesting pet experience.

Small animals, such as guinea pigs, hamsters, and rabbits, are popular pets for those with limited space or who are looking for a low-maintenance pet. They are social creatures that require daily interaction and attention, but they are easy to care for and make great first-time pets. Small animals can be easily trained and they provide their owners with a variety of fun and interactive experiences.

There are many different types of pets to choose from, each with its own unique personality and characteristics. Whether you are looking for a loyal companion, a low-maintenance pet, or an exotic and interesting creature, there is a pet out there that is perfect for you. Understanding the different types of pets available can help you make an informed decision about which type of pet is right for you and your lifestyle.One of the most important aspects of pet ownership is understanding pet behavior. Each pet species has its own unique behavior patterns and body language, and it is important to understand these in order to create a strong and healthy bond with your pet. By learning about your pet's natural instincts, you can create an environment that is comfortable and safe for them, and you can avoid potential conflicts and misunderstandings.Pet behavior can be influenced by a number of factors, including genetics, environment, and socialization. For example, some dogs are naturally more aggressive than others, while some cats are naturally more independent. Understanding the factors that influence pet behavior can help you identify potential problem areas and take steps to address them.Pet body language is another important aspect of understanding pet behavior. Animals communicate through a variety of physical cues, such as posture, facial expressions, and vocalizations. By learning to interpret these cues, you can gain a better understanding of how your pet is feeling and what they are trying to communicate. For example, a wagging tail in a dog often indicates excitement or friendliness, while a stiff posture and flattened ears may indicate fear or aggression.It is important to note that pets can also display behaviors that are not natural, but are instead learned or develop as a result of their environment. These behaviors can range from destructive chewing or digging, to aggression towards other pets or people. In order to address these behaviors, it is important to understand the underlying cause, and to work with a pet behaviorist or trainer to find a solution.Understanding pet behavior is an important aspect of pet ownership. By learning about your pet's natural instincts, body language, and behavior patterns, you can create a strong and healthy bond with your pet, and ensure that they live a happy and fulfilling life. By taking the time to understand your pet's behavior, you can become a better pet owner and provide your pet with the best possible care.Bonding with your pet is also an important aspect of pet ownership. A strong bond between you and your pet can provide them with a sense of security, comfort, and love. It can also make your relationship with your pet more enjoyable and fulfilling, and can even improve your own mental and physical health.Bonding with your pet can take time and effort, but it is well worth it. One of the most important things you can do to bond with your pet is to spend time with them. This can include playing, grooming, and taking them for walks. During these activities, be sure to give your pet plenty of attention and affection, and try to get to know their unique personality and behavior patterns.

In addition to spending time with your pet, it is also important to provide them with plenty of positive reinforcement. This can include giving them treats, praise, and affection when they display good behavior. This will help to strengthen the bond between you and your pet, and will encourage them to continue to display good behavior.Another way to bond with your pet is to engage in activities together, such as training sessions, agility courses, or obedience classes. These activities not only provide a fun and positive bonding experience, but also help to keep your pet mentally and physically stimulated.It is important to remember that bonding with your pet is a two-way street. As you build a stronger bond with your pet, they will also become more attached to you. This can result in a more loving and harmonious relationship, and can provide both you and your.Bonding with your pet is an important aspect of pet ownership. By spending time with your pet, providing positive reinforcement, and engaging in activities together, you can build a strong and loving bond with your pet that will provide both you and your pet with a sense of comfort and security.

CHAPTER THREE

Essential Pet Care

Providing your pet with proper care is essential for their overall health and well-being. Feeding and nutrition, exercise and playtime, grooming, and health care are all key components of essential pet care.

Starting with feeding and nutrition, it is important to choose a balanced and nutritious diet that meets your pet's specific nutritional needs. This may include a commercially available pet food, or a home-prepared diet. It is also important to be mindful of portion sizes and to avoid overfeeding, as pets can easily become overweight.

Exercise and playtime are also important for your pet's physical and mental health. Regular physical activity can help to keep your pet in shape, reduce stress and anxiety, and strengthen the bond between you and your pet. This can include activities such as walks, runs, and games of fetch, as well as more structured exercise and training sessions.Grooming is another important aspect of pet care, and can help to keep your pet healthy and looking their best. This may include regular brushing, bathing, and nail trims, as well as maintaining proper dental hygiene. Grooming can also help to keep your pet comfortable, and can help to prevent skin and coat problems.Finally, health care is an essential component of pet care. This includes regular check-ups and vaccinations, as well as prompt treatment of any health issues that may arise. By staying proactive and vigilant about your pet's health, you can help to keep them happy and healthy for years to come.

In conclusion, providing your pet with proper care is essential for their overall health and well-being. Feeding and nutrition, exercise and playtime, grooming, and health care are all key components of essential pet care, and should be prioritized by all pet owners. By taking the time to care for your pet, you can help to ensure that they live a long, healthy, and happy life.

CHAPTER FOUR

Training and Behavioral Issues

Training your pet is an essential part of responsible pet ownership. Basic obedience training helps to create a well-behaved pet and strengthen the bond between you and your pet. Common behavioral problems such as barking, chewing, and digging can be effectively dealt with through positive reinforcement training techniques and consistent behavior management. Preventing destructive behavior is key in protecting your home and belongings, as well as ensuring the safety of your pet. With patience, persistence, and proper training techniques, you can help your pet overcome behavior problems and develop into a well-behaved companion.

In addition to basic obedience training, it's also important to consider socialization training for your pet. Socialization is the process of exposing your pet to different people, places, and experiences in a positive and controlled manner. This helps to prevent fearfulness and aggression, and encourages good behavior in different environments. It's important to start socialization training early in a pet's life, but it's never too late to start.

Another aspect of training and behavioral issues is addressing specific behaviors that may be problematic for you or your pet. For example, if your pet has separation anxiety, a behavior modification plan can be put in place to help reduce anxiety and increase independence. If your pet has a fear of certain stimuli, such as loud noises or vacuum cleaners, counter-conditioning techniques can be used to help change the pet's emotional response to the stimulus.

Proper training and addressing behavioral issues can lead to a happier and more harmonious relationship between you and your pet. Consistent training and positive reinforcement techniques can help create a well-behaved pet and enhance the bond between you and your companion.It's also important to note that not all behavior issues can be resolved through training alone. In some cases, underlying medical conditions such as pain, sensory deficits, or cognitive decline can contribute to behavioral issues. In these instances, a veterinarian should be consulted to rule out any medical causes and provide a proper diagnosis.It's also important to seek professional help if you're unable to effectively address your pet's behavior problems on your own. A certified professional dog trainer or animal behaviorist can provide guidance and support to help you and your pet overcome any behavioral challenges. They can also develop a customized training plan that takes into account your pet's unique needs and personality.In addition to seeking professional help, it's also important to remain patient and persistent in your training efforts. Changing long-standing behaviors takes time and effort, and setbacks are a normal part of the process. It's important to remain consistent in your training efforts and to never use punishment or physical force as a training method. Instead, focus on positive reinforcement techniques and consistent behavior management to help your pet succeed.

CHAPTER FIVE

Creating a Safe and Happy Home

When it comes to creating a safe and happy home for your pet, it's important to consider the type of environment that's best suited to your pet's needs. For example, some pets may thrive in a larger home with a spacious yard, while others may do better in a smaller apartment with minimal outdoor space. Consider your pet's breed, size, and personality when choosing the right living environment.Once you've chosen the right environment, it's important to make sure your home is safe and comfortable for your pet. This includes making sure that all potential hazards, such as toxic plants or sharp objects, are removed or secured. You should also ensure that your home is well-ventilated, that your pet has access to fresh water at all times, and that your pet's sleeping and resting areas are comfortable and free from draft.In addition to providing a safe and comfortable home, it's also important to keep your pet entertained. This can be done through interactive toys, puzzles, and other engaging activities. Regular playtime and exercise are also important to keep your pet physically and mentally stimulated. Providing mental stimulation can help prevent boredom, reduce destructive behavior, and enhance the bond between you and your pet.

In conclusion, creating a safe and happy home is an important aspect of responsible pet ownership. By considering your pet's needs, providing a safe and comfortable environment, and keeping your pet entertained, you can help your pet thrive in their home and lead a happy and healthy life.

CHAPTER SIX

Pet-Friendly Activities

Pet-friendly activities can help build a strong bond between pet owners and their pets, while also providing much-needed exercise and mental stimulation for pets. In this chapter, we will explore different types of pet-friendly activities, including outdoor adventures, indoor activities, and pet-friendly travel.

Outdoor Adventures

There are many outdoor activities that pet owners can enjoy with their pets, such as hiking, camping, and swimming. These activities provide a great opportunity for pets to experience the great outdoors, interact with nature, and get some exercise. However, pet owners must always be mindful of their pet's safety and ensure that they are properly prepared for the activity, including providing enough food and water, bringing a first-aid kit, and making sure that their pet is wearing a collar with identification tags.

Indoor Activities

For pet owners who prefer indoor activities, there are many options available, such as playing fetch, training, and puzzle toys. Indoor activities can also provide mental stimulation and help prevent destructive behavior. Some popular indoor activities include playing hide-and-seek, training sessions, and interactive toys, such as puzzle feeders, that challenge pets to use their minds.

Pet-Friendly Travel

Traveling with your pet can be a great way to bond and create new memories together. However, pet-friendly travel requires careful planning and preparation to ensure that both pet and owner have a safe and enjoyable experience. Pet owners should research pet-friendly accommodations, make sure their pet is up-to-date on all necessary vaccinations, and carry proof of vaccination with them. They should also plan for any necessary pit stops and bring along plenty of food, water, and any necessary medications for their pet.

Pet-friendly activities provide a great opportunity for pet owners to bond with their pets and help keep them physically and mentally stimulated. From outdoor adventures to indoor activities, and pet-friendly travel, there is a wealth of options available for pet owners to choose from. The most important thing is to always prioritize your pet's safety and well-being, and to have fun while enjoying the journey together.

CHAPTER SEVEN

Coping with the Loss of a Pet

Losing a pet can be a devastating experience, and it is common to feel overwhelmed by feelings of sadness, grief, and loss. It is important to understand that grieving the loss of a pet is a normal and natural process, and that it is okay to take the time you need to heal. There are several steps you can take to help yourself cope with the loss of a pet: Allow yourself to feel your emotions: It is natural to feel a range of emotions after losing a pet, including sadness, anger, guilt, and even relief. Allow yourself to feel and express these emotions in a healthy way, whether it's through talking to friends or family members, writing in a journal, or seeking support from a pet loss support group. Memorialize your pet: There are many different ways to memorialize your pet, from creating a special photo album or memorial garden, to writing a letter or poem in their honor. Find a way to honor your pet's memory that feels meaningful to you. Seek support: Coping with the loss of a pet can be a difficult and isolating experience, but it's important to remember that you don't have to go through it alone. Seek support from friends and family members, or consider joining a pet loss support group where you can connect with others who are also grieving. Take care of yourself: Taking care of yourself both physically and emotionally is essential during the grieving process. This may include getting enough sleep, eating well, and engaging in activities that bring you joy and comfort. Celebrate the life of your pet: Rather than focusing solely on the loss, take time to celebrate the life of your pet and the special moments you shared together. This may involve sharing stories with others or simply reflecting on the love and joy your pet brought into your life. Losing a pet can be one of the hardest experiences a pet owner will face, but with time and support, it is possible to heal and find peace in the memories of your beloved companion

CHAPTER EIGHT

Conclusion

Pet care is a complex and rewarding experience that requires time, effort, and dedication. Whether you are a new pet owner or have been caring for your furry friend for years, it is important to understand the various aspects of pet care, from feeding and nutrition, to training and behavioral issues, and everything in between.It is also important to remember that your pet's health and happiness depend on creating a safe and happy home environment, as well as engaging in pet-friendly activities that allow them to express their natural instincts and explore the world around them.As a pet owner, it is also important to understand and cope with the loss of a pet, and to seek support and find healthy ways to memorialize and celebrate their life.In closing, pet care is a journey filled with joy, love, and companionship. We encourage all pet owners to continue their pet-loving journey, and to never stop learning and growing as a responsible and caring pet parent.

Top of Form

End Matter

In conclusion, pet ownership is a rewarding and fulfilling experience that brings joy, love, and companionship into our lives. With the information and advice provided in this book, you will be well equipped to care for your pet and ensure a happy and healthy life for both of you. So, let's embark on this journey together and discover the many wonders of pet care.

Printed by Libri Plureos GmbH in Hamburg,
Germany

9 798889 753100